Americas Future Paying Higher Taxes

America's Future

How You Will Pay Higher Taxes

Billy Grinslott

Billy Grinslott

Americas Future Paying Higher Taxes

Copyright © Billy Grinslott
All rights reserved.
ISBN: 9798746576262
Billy Grinslott

Americas Future Paying Higher Taxes

DEDICATION

This book is dedicated to all the great Americans, that still believe that the United States is a great place to live.

All the great Americans who still believe that we need to protect our constitution, our heritage, and our way of life.

To everyone who is struggling, hope for a brighter future.

Billy Grinslott

Americas Future Paying Higher Taxes

Billy Grinslott

Americas Future Paying Higher Taxes

CONTENTS

Acknowledgements i

CHAPTERS

1	Introduction	Pg # 3
2	Constitution	Pg # 4
3	Give Your Paycheck Away	Pg # 9
4	Goodbye Savings, Retirement	Pg # 24
5	Work Until You Die	Pg # 28
6	No Jobs and Poverty	Pg # 32
7	Voting Rights	Pg # 37
8	Climate Change	Pg # 40
9	Immigration	Pg # 44
10	Overpopulation	Pg # 48
11	Starvation, Food Shortages	Pg # 49
12	Pandemics, Diseases, Viruses	Pg # 52
13	Gun Violence, Protection	Pg # 55
14	Race Riots, Wars Among us	Pg # 64
15	Cops or no Cops.	Pg # 68
16	Packing the Supreme Court	Pg # 79
17	Downfall of America	Pg # 80

Billy Grinslott

Americas Future Paying Higher Taxes

Americas Future Paying Higher Taxes

ACKNOWLEDGMENTS

Thanks to Dustin Michael, Devan Brandt, Kinsey Marie, Robyn Kelly, Julie Berg for all their insight and Help.

Americas Future Paying Higher Taxes

Americas Future Paying Higher Taxes

Introduction

What if I told you that within the next few years you will be paying more and higher taxes than you've ever seen in America. That there's a plan where your whole paycheck will end up going to the Government. What if I told you that the plan is already underway? Would you believe me. Well, it's true.

What if I told you that your savings and investment accounts will be taxed at the highest rate on capital gains. What if I told you that they are going to raise the estate tax and lower the amount that an estate can give to its beneficiaries. Would you believe me, well it's true?

What if I told you, that your savings and retirement accounts would be taken from you? What if I told you that there would be no such thing as retirement, you would have to work until you die? Would you believe me. Well, it's true.

What if I told you, they have a plan to dismantle the constitution to make this happen? Once they dismantle the constitution, they will easily control every aspect of your life. That includes raising taxes, taking your paycheck, savings, and retirement.

What if I told you, they had a plan to take away your voting rights? What if I told you the reason was so they can select who will run the country as dictatorship to control you. Would you believe me, it's true?

This Book will give you all the details, along with many other topics that are already affecting America and will affect its future.

Topics include.
Taxes and more taxes.
How your whole paycheck will be taken away.
How your savings and retirement will be gone.
How you will work until you die.
High unemployment, no jobs, living in poverty.
Voting Rights, how they will be taken away.
Gun rights, protecting guns, why you will need one.
Cops or no Cops. Police defunding & dismantling.
Protecting the Constitution, why you will need it.
Immigration, how it affects America.
Overpopulation of America.
Starvation and food shortages.
Pandemics, future pandemics.
Climate change. How it will change life on earth.
Race riots, Systemic racism, and wars among us.
The downfall of America. How it will collapse.

US Constitution

We're going to start this book off by talking about the constitution. Why, because it's the most important document we have, to protect our rights. Without the constitution, we have no way to stand up for ourselves.

The constitution was created to keep the government and other organizations from imposing their will onto the American people. It was created so the American people would have a say in how their country is run.

Without the constitution all our rights and liberty will be taken away. To protect ourselves from having everything in our daily life controlled, we must protect the constitution.

Right now, in America our constitution is under attack. Now we could sit back and say that the government wants to destroy our constitution. So, they can control every aspect of our lives, but it's not just them. There are some politicians that do believe in this and others that don't.

We have some good politicians that still believe that America should be run by the people and the government should do what's best for the people. But we have other politicians that believe in completely controlling every aspect of our lives.

How well America does, isn't in their best interest. They want the power to control you and the best way to do it, is to take away your rights, by getting rid of the constitution. They are out for power and not prosperity, but they're alone.

For the ones that do believe in eliminating the constitution, they're going to go to extreme lengths to make it happen. They have a personal agenda and they're going to fulfill it, at whatever cost.

Some politicians have sold their sole to the devil. Here's one thing I want you to remember about some politicians. They are bought and paid for.

Now, what do I mean when I say they are bought and paid for. You must look at a politician's life to understand it. They don't get into office without accepting money from certain people, groups, organizations, or companies. To get elected they must run a campaign. Those campaign funds come from somewhere.

The American people do donate. We figure that if we donate to a certain candidate that they will run the country the way we want once they are elected. It usually doesn't turn out that way. There's one main reason for that.

Politicians make promises and offer certain things to get elected. Once elected it seems that they completely forget about the promises they made to the people and run off with their own personal agendas. Or to fulfill the agendas of the organizations or companies that donated to them.

Certain groups, organizations and companies donate a ton of money to get their representative elected. Why you may ask, they have laws they want changed to benefit them. They have special interests they need and who better to make that happen than a politician.

So, what some politicians end up doing is forgetting about the citizens and they cater to the organizations and companies that paid their way into government. They end up doing backdoor deals that benefit themselves, these companies, and organizations.

What's happened over time is, you now have politicians that are owned by these organizations and companies. So instead of doing what's best for the

Americas Future Paying Higher Taxes

people, they do what's best for them. You ever heard the expression, don't bite the hand that feeds you.

Have you ever wondered how some politicians become so wealthy while in office? That's because there's a lot of back door deals going on that benefit them and these organizations or companies. Along the way, they're lining their pockets with your tax dollars.

So, what's ended up happening over time is a lot of corruption has taken place in our government. Some of our elected officials have decided to climb in bed with these organizations and companies.

How does this affect our country and the constitution? When it comes to our country, it's no longer being run by our government. It's being run by a lot of rich people, organizations and companies that have bought off certain politicians.

The issue is these rich people, organizations and companies want complete control over the country. There are some politicians that are on board with them and together they want control over everything. They are going to do whatever is needed to accomplish this.

Let me give you an example. As I said, not every politician thinks this way. In the 2020 presidential election we had a president running for his 2nd term. He was president from 2016 to 2020. That was Donald Trump.

One of his motto's was, I'm going to drain the swamp. What he meant by this was he was going to get rid of the corruption in our government and turn the government back over to the people.

From the minute he took office, the battle was underway. The politicians that are used to benefitting from all this corruption were not happy. Their livelyhood was at stake. So, they ganged up on him. They also managed to get a lot of organizations to back them. Why, because they all have the same goals.

The bottom line is this. The only reason they wanted him out of office is because he stood up for the American people and wanted to give the country back to the people. He wanted to end the government corruption.

Well, that didn't fit in with their plan. Where are they going to get their next meal from if they can't use the taxpayers to benefit from.

During the 2020 presidential election, they pulled every battleship out and went on full attack. They got everyone involved to do whatever it took to make sure he didn't get re-elected. The problem is they deceived and lied to the American public and changed voting laws to make it happen.

Now, why did I bring all this up. Because it's not just some politicians you have to worry about. There's organizations and companies that have the same agenda. They all want to control every aspect of your life. They want to run the country how they see fit, and your rights don't matter.

This means that when it comes to protecting the constitution, we must battle all these organizations along with the politicians that are on board with taking over our country.

Americas Future Paying Higher Taxes

This plan to control every aspect of your life, just didn't pop up overnight. The plan was started several years ago and has been in progression since. Over the next few years, it's going to rapidly be put into place.

They have several ways and things they must do to accomplish their plan and it's underway. They are coming for everything you have. The constitution is not the only thing they want control of.

What I do know is once they dismantle or do away with the constitution, everything else you have will be gone. Crunch time is upon us, if we don't protect the constitution, our life, liberty, and way of life will be gone. Along with everything else you have.

This book will discuss all the ways they plan on taking over the country, along with our last line of defense for the constitution. It will also discuss many more topics that are affecting us right now and will get worse in America's future.

Once you've read the full book, it will make sense. One last note before we move on. America is supposed to be run by the people, not the government and other entities. The time has come for us to take an interest in protecting our way of life. We are being sold out to the highest bidder.

Give Your Paycheck to the Government

Let's talk about everybody's favorite subject, money. Ooh, money, money, money. I'm going to ask you some questions, please participate by thinking seriously about them. I'm also going to ask you to be honest with yourself, when thinking about these.

We're going to talk about how you will end up giving your whole paycheck to the government. Now you might think this is ridiculous. By the time we are done with this chapter, you may have a different outlook.

One of the biggest problems we have in the United States right now is our debt is way too high. What do you think our current deficit is in the United States? The answer is around $28 trillion. At the time I am writing this, now that's going to change because we keep racking up more debt. So, it's only going to increase.

First question, who do you think is responsible for running the deficit up so high? The answer might not be what you want to hear. Think about that for a minute. But it's going to be, the truth.

Next question. Who do you think should pay off the deficit? One of the only ways that the deficit gets paid off, is by raising taxes. Now, I'm willing to bet there's some people sitting there right now saying, not me, don't raise my taxes. We can get somebody else to pay for it.

Next question. When they raise taxes on everybody, making an income of over $400,000, do you think, you're not affected by it, because you make less than that.

I'm going to ask you to keep an open mind when I make this statement. I'm going to be brutally honest.

Americas Future Paying Higher Taxes

Part of the problem we have, is we aren't always honest with ourselves? We usually want to blame something or someone else for the problems we have.

I'm going to ask you to think about what I have to say here with an open mind. You might not like it, but it will make sense. The problem with telling the truth is, nobody really wants to hear it.

I also realize that, in society, when somebody does tell the truth. They are automatically labeled, yelled at, screamed at, belittled or the trump card is pulled out and they are called racist. Because somebody does not agree with them. I'm going to ask you to not do that. It should not happen anyway. We should be able to share opinions without all that nonsense. As you read this book. Please keep that in mind.

A lot of people want to blame the government for running up the debt. Yes, they are to blame for a lot of it. They do spend money foolishly and they seem to use the taxpayers to line their own pockets and the companies and organizations who own them. Also, to fulfill their own personal agendas.

Not to mention every time they pass a bill there seems to be a lot of money going to places it should not go. They use the American people's money for their own personal agendas.

Every time there's a problem, we want to blame the government. But it's not completely their fault. Now don't get me wrong, they do their share of overspending and allotting money to places it shouldn't go.

But sometimes when they hand out money or do

bailouts, it's because the people or companies need it or have asked for it. So, they are only trying to do their jobs and keep the people happy.

Let's answer the first question. Who do you think is responsible for running up the debt in the United States? The answer is you. Me, everybody, all of us. I know you are shaking your head a little bit. But we are all at fault for running up our national debt. It is our country, and we allow it to happen.

So. Let me clear this up. It's our fault because we allow our government to take advantage of us. Every time they pass a bill and money is used for non-legitimate reasons; we just accept it.

Instead of standing up to the government and telling them to stop spending our money foolishly or for their own personal agendas. Or to pad the pockets of other organizations or companies that benefit, we just let it happen. We accept it as normal and don't control how our money is spent.

Plenty of people have been taking advantage of the government for a long time. We've got people that have been on assistance that probably should not be an assistance. Do not get me wrong, I don't think anybody in the United States has a problem helping people that do need assistance. We are good people that way.

Let's look at where we are at fault. There's a lot of people that take advantage of the system. You might ask why I'm bringing this up, it's because it runs up our deficit. We live in what I would like to call a free society. I do not mean that we are free. I mean everybody wants

Americas Future Paying Higher Taxes

something for free.

I want free schooling. I want free healthcare. What else can I get for free? Give me something for free. The problem is nothing is free. Somebody must pay for it. But when it comes time to pay it back. They do not want to pay it back. They want somebody else to pay it back for them. Isn't it everyone's responsibility?

Not only do we have individuals taking advantage of the government. We have organizations and companies that are taking money and do not really need it. We have states that cannot control their own deficits, they want money from the government. Everyone has their hand in the cookie jar.

Now we're all guilty of allowing this to happen. Because we have the attitude that, well, money is free. They can just print more. We allow this to happen. So, America needs to come together and stop spending so much money.

The other problem we have is, every time something happens in America, we expect the government to bail us out. Typically, this is in forms of money or stimulus checks. We've gotten to the point that it is normal to do this. It has become the norm for Americans.

To sum it all up, what I'm trying to say is, it has become normal for American people to hold their hand out every time something happens and say, give me, give me, give me. The problem is most Americans don't think there is a consequence to this action, but there is.

We've been programmed as Americans, to spend

money. We've gotten accustomed to it. Most Americans run around with the attitude. That we can just spend, spend, spend. You can only spend so much money before that debt must be paid back. It's no different than owning a credit card. There's a limit and then it must be paid back.

The deficit is no different. We can only rack up the deficit so much, then it is going to have to be paid back. Since we all took part in racking up the debt. It will be up to all of us to pay it back. Don't get me wrong, our elected officials do their share of overspending and fulfilling personal agendas, but we allow it to happen.

We as Americans have had the attitude that I want the best, no matter what the cost. We have been programmed to spend, spend, spend. That attitude must change. We need to run the government like we run our households, on a tight budget.

Now like I said, the truth hurts. The fact is we are all guilty of running up the country's debt. We allow it to happen and the only way it will change is if we let our government know that it needs to stop.

I want to say, before I get on with this. My heart goes out to everyone that was affected by COVID-19. We personally lost a family member because of it and have had family members get sick. We have had another family member that has been unemployed since it started. So, we've all been affected by it.

I'm going to give you an example and it may not be the best example. But Covid-19 has raised the debt in the United States, quite a bit. Now don't get me wrong.

Americas Future Paying Higher Taxes

No one asked for Covid-19 to be here, and a lot of us went through a hard time.

But what's going to happen next is, everybody is going to use Covid-19 as an excuse for why our deficit is so high and it is just simply not true. Granted, it did raise our deficit.

The reason I bring this up is, because before COVID-19, we already had a huge deficit. We were already used to spending money like gangbusters. So, we can't use Covid-19 as the only excuse of why our deficit is so high.

Here's some numbers. At the end of 2019, our national debt was around $22 trillion. This is before Covid-19 hit the country. Our average debt goes up $2 to $3 trillion a year. So, even without covid-19, our debt would have been around $25 trillion by 2021.

Our deficit would have still gone up even if Covid-19 were here or not. It may not have gone up as much as it did. But like I said, Americans are accustomed to spending money and the deficit still would have gone up. We would still have a huge deficit.

I'm not going to carry on with that for too long, you got the point. What I want you to ask yourself is an honest question. When the Government handed out stimulus checks for Covid-19, did you spend it to pay your bills?

The government handed out the stimulus checks because that was their intention. They knew people were falling behind on their mortgages and bills. So, they created the stimulus checks to help people pay their debt. It's what everyone asked for and wanted. We as a nation asked for help.

You might think, do I work for the government, I don't work for the government. But the government, did what the people asked them to do. That was to give you money to help you pay your bills. That's just being honest. Once again, we allowed them to borrow more money than what was needed.

For those of you who spent your stimulus check to pay your mortgage or bills, kudos to you. You spent the money on what it was intended for, way to go.

But what happened instead was, a lot of people went out shopping, take a deep breath, relax, I'm not accusing everyone. They spent their stimulus check to go on a shopping spree and it was not to buy food or pay off their bills. At this point you might be laughing, screaming, yelling or you might think I am an idiot. But I can prove it

I own four websites. I know a lot of people that also run businesses. What is odd, is our sales increased drastically right after stimulus checks were handed out. This tells me a lot of people really didn't use the money to pay their bills. But they took the money and went out shopping.

I can also verify this because, we take phone orders. I had a guy specifically tell me on the phone, that he got his stimulus check and he had to spend it. My first thought was, well you're supposed to use that money to pay your bills, so we can lessen the burden on the economy. Oh well.

Americas Future Paying Higher Taxes

Now, I don't mean to be harsh on this, but I am trying to make a point. A lot of people took money and did not do what they were supposed to do with it. There's part of that, I want something for free.

So, let me prove my point again about human nature and not everyone is to blame. Here's what's going to happen next. All the people that took the money and didn't use it to pay their bills, are still going to be behind on their bills and mortgage.

Then they're going to be looking at the government to bail them out again. They're going to be asking for another stimulus check. This will raise our deficit even more. Because they didn't use the money as it was intended.

Like I said, I was going to be brutally honest. Don't get angry at me. Sometimes telling the truth hurts. But these are the facts. They didn't pay their bills and they will be asking for more money. As you are sitting here reading this, you must ask yourself the honest question. What did you do with your stimulus check?

Now I know using Covid-19 may have been a bad example. The only reason I used it, is because it was one of the latest events where we asked the government for money. My point is with or without Covid-19. The American people will always find ways to spend money and ask for a bailout. We've gotten used to it.

We've been doing it for a long time. We've been racking up debt for a long time. We've gotten accustomed to it. The problem is that debt is our debt, and it must be paid back.

We've got this attitude, that we know the debt must be paid back, but when it comes time to raise taxes to pay off the debt. Everyone starts playing a game hide and seek. Not me, don't find me, find someone else. Make somebody else pay it. It's not my responsibility, actually it is.

I asked the question before. If they raise taxes on everybody, making over $400,000 a year. Will it affect you? The answer is a straight out yes.

Here's how. When you raise taxes on anybody in the United States. It creates a trickledown effect. When you raise taxes on people or companies making over $400,000 a year. Trust me, I don't make over $400,000 a year. But I'm wise enough to understand what is going to happen next.

To recuperate the extra money that they're paying in taxes. They will either raise prices on their products, or layoff people? Either way, it trickles down. Not to mention, that some companies will move out of the country. Which will Cause more unemployment. It will also affect wages, you will be paid less, so they can recuperate the cost.

When you raise taxes on big companies, they're going to pass that expense down to you. So, in the long run, you are paying more for everything you buy. They're going to get it from you, by raising their prices.

The next time you go shopping, if you pay more for a product, think about this and it will make sense. The bottom line is whether they raise your taxes or somebody else's taxes. It has a trickledown effect, and it

Americas Future Paying Higher Taxes

affects everybody.

So, let me give you another example. Recently they shut down the Keystone Pipeline. Lots of people got laid off. It's not just the fact that Keystone laid people off. It affects all the other businesses that were relying on money coming in. Those businesses are going to have to lay people off because they have less money. Lots of people lost their jobs and income. So, as you see, there's a trickledown effect.

What happened next, was gas prices went up almost immediately? My propane prices went up by over $0.50 a gallon. Like I said, there's a trickledown effect to everything that happens. As a consumer, you will pay more for your product's.

If you pay more on gas, heating, and electrical bills, now you know why. Raising taxes and doing away with jobs, does affect everyone. It doesn't matter who you raise the taxes on, it affects everybody.

Let's talk a little more about human nature and the willingness of some individuals who want to take advantage of the system, no matter what the cost is. Let's talk about unemployment. During the Covid-19 pandemic, the government raised and extended the amount of unemployment insurance to help people who lost their jobs.

My opinion on unemployment is we need it. Plenty of people lose their jobs for unexpected reasons and help is needed. I think we all agree on that. The point behind unemployment is it's there to help you till you can get back to work.

Billy Grinslott

We've pretty much worked through the Covid-19 pandemic and everything is returning to normal for most people. The only ones that aren't going back to normal are the ones that still want to use Covid-19 as an excuse.

Jobs are coming back strong, and companies are hiring. Yet we've got individuals out there that refuse to go back to work and are taking advantage of the system, because they are making more on unemployment.

Rather than go back to work and lessen the load on the economy, they've decided to take advantage of the system. Whether unemployment is paid by the employer or reimbursed through the government, everyone will end up paying for it.

When the employer must pay higher unemployment insurance, they're going to pass that cost on to the consumer. You will pay more for everything. Not to mention it will affect wages, you will be earning less.

Now let's get to the point. Being that we as Americans have this carefree attitude when it comes to spending money, and we keep racking up our deficit. That debt is going to have to be paid off. We can only run the deficit up so much before it must be paid off.

The only way to pay off the deficit, is to raise taxes. Taxes will have to be raised, on everyone. Here's what's going to happen. Taxes will be raised on everyone. Of course, the government will have more money. But it will not be used to pay off the deficit. It will be used just to pay the monthly bill on the debt we already have.

Americas Future Paying Higher Taxes

Understand this, the government borrows money to keep the economy going. No different than if you borrow money, and you must pay the bill. The government borrows money and it's our job to pay that bill every month. This is done through taxation.

Since we're only paying the monthly bill on the debt we owe, the deficit doesn't go down. Since we're only paying the monthly bill and we are used to spending and borrowing money, the deficit will continue to rise. So, the deficit will still be going up because we are only paying the monthly bill on the debt we have.

To keep up with the payment on the debt we owe, and the rising deficit, taxes will have to be raised again. Now, I'm not going to keep repeating this, the cycle continues this way. Deficit keeps going up, we have higher debt to pay, more taxes need to be collected to pay that debt, and that cycle continues.

Eventually, you will be taxed so much, that you will have nothing left in your paycheck. It will all be going to help pay off the debt that we have accumulated. Hence, you will be giving your whole paycheck to the government to help pay the debt, through taxation.

Now, I realize that there's some people that would be perfectly happy with turning their paycheck over every week and getting everything paid for. But I believe most people want to keep their paycheck and spend money on what they want to.

If we all don't come together and get a handle on the country's debt, this is what we must look forward to in the future. One last note before we move on.

Billy Grinslott

There's been a lot of talk about turning our country in a socialist or communist country. What do you think happens? You go to work; you give your paycheck to the government. They give you a house to live in, they give you an allowance to live on. If we don't control our debt, eventually there will be no choice.

Now for some people, this may be ok. I still think most people want the freedom to spend their paycheck how they see fit. The only way out of this, is for all of us to come together and stop spending foolishly and stop running up the deficit.

We need to come together and make it clear to our government that spending money foolishly needs to stop. It's our government and they should do what the people want. If we keep allowing it, it's only going to get worse.

Besides being taxed out of your paycheck, there's a couple of things to consider. First, it's been mentioned that certain people or organizations are intentionally driving up the debt, so they can push their agenda of turning the US into a socialist or communist country.

They already have a plan in place to confiscate your paycheck. Their goal is to have everyone turn their paycheck over to them and they will decide how you live.

The point is there's certain people that want to control every aspect of your life. They don't care about you. For them it's all about power and money. They want it all and they will do whatever it takes. They want to run the country their way and your opinion doesn't

Americas Future Paying Higher Taxes

matter.

Let me prove a point. I started this book off by talking about politicians selling their sole. They owe the organizations and companies that got them elected. Did you ever notice when they borrow money to do a stimulus check, that most of money doesn't go to the people?

A two trillion-dollar package and a small percent went out in stimulus checks. Where do think the rest of that money went. You guessed it, to personal agendas, or to the people that own them.

On top of that they used the American people's emotion to make it happen. I've got no problem with handing out stimulus checks to people that need help.

The problem is this. We should have stood up as a whole and told our government to just borrow enough money for the stimulus checks, but we didn't. We allowed them to run our deficit up by the trillions to fulfill their own personal agendas.

We have the right to dictate how our government spends our money, but we don't. Instead, we allow them to use our money to line their pockets or other organizations and run up the deficit.

Some politicians fought against doing this. They said there was too much padding in it, the money was not being used for its intentions. Of course, the people went into an uproar, I want my check, I want my money now. No matter what the cost.

My point is, we didn't control the spending at the time. We lived for the moment. As the deficit rises and we aren't taking an interest in how our money is spent or controlling our budget. The moment will come where they ask for your paycheck to pay off the deficit.

Don't whine or complain, just hand it over, because you didn't take an interest in controlling the spending at the time. We will all have to pay for it at some point. We have the right to dictate how our money is spent and we aren't doing it.

Let's talk about the green new deal. The current administration is planning on borrowing 6 to 10 trillion dollars to make this happen. Who do you think is going to be responsible for paying this back?

It won't be big companies, for two reasons. One when they are taxed, they will pass that expense down to the consumer. Two, some companies will leave the US putting the burden back on the taxpayers. That means all of us will be paying that debt back through taxation. No matter what they tell you, it always trickles down to the taxpayers.

Finally, they are working on passing a bill where they are going to raise the capital gains taxes on savings and retirement accounts. This is a tax on everyone, told you not to believe them when they said they were just raising taxes on the wealthy.

In this bill they are also raising the death tax, known as the estate tax. Here's what I never understood about the death tax. That money has already been taxed. Well, we're used to double, triple taxation. The point is they are coming after everyone in one way or another.

Americas Future Paying Higher Taxes

The other reason you may be asked to give up your paycheck is because of equality. We'll cover that in the next chapter. The bottom line is, if we don't take an interest in controlling our country's debt, we will all have to pay the piper. Taxes, Taxes, Taxes. Yeeha.

Goodbye Savings & Retirement

Now I'm not going to spend much time on this subject. It ties in with giving your whole paycheck to the government. There's a couple reason why you might have to say goodbye to your savings and retirement.

A few years ago, one of the things that popped up was, the idea of dipping into people's retirement and savings accounts to help pay off the deficit. The idea was immediately shut down because of who was president at the time.

In the last chapter we discovered how it's possible that you will be giving your whole paycheck to the government through taxation, socialism, or communism. Because we ran the deficit up so high. The same rule applies here.

Once our debt goes up so high and your paycheck is gone due to taxation. To pay off the debt we have accumulated, we will be asked to give up what we have in our savings and retirement accounts to keep the country running. Now I'm sure a lot of people would be upset by this.

You might think that this would never happen or

that there's no way it can happen. I'm here to tell you that it will eventually happen, if we don't straighten out the debt we have in our country. Once the constitution is dismantled, you will have no more rights or protection. They will pass whatever laws they need.

Here's the problem you have. The seed has already been planted in the minds of many. Once a seed is planted, it starts to grow. It eventually blossoms into a full-grown plant. In this case it will be an ugly weed no one likes. The point is the seed has been planted and in will mature into something real, it always does.

Another thing to consider. Right now, in the united states, we have a lot of division going on. Some of our population believes that everybody should be equal or have equality. Others still believe that we have a right to succeed, gain wealth and live the American dream.

The American dream has always been freedom. The freedom to make as much money as you want. The freedom to spend your money how you see fit. The freedom to accumulate wealth. The freedom to succeed.

But, like I said, we have many people that think we should all be equal or have equality. What I mean by this, is, we should all own the same house, drive the same car, have the same amount of money. This topic has been popping up a lot lately.

Equality means each individual or group of people is given the same resources or opportunities. The number of people that believe in equality is growing. As it grows, more people are jumping on board.

So, what this means for all the people who have

Americas Future Paying Higher Taxes

managed to gain wealth, you will be asked to give up your money, so we can all be equal or have equality. Oh, that includes your paycheck, told you I would tie it together. Now this doesn't seem fair, but a lot of people think it is fair. Why should one person have more than the other.

Now, the problem with equality is, it ruins the economy. Let me explain. Let's say you're one of those individuals who works 60 hours a week because you have the drive to succeed. You put money away, so you can have savings, retire early, or have a good retirement.

Once you lose all that money, your drive to work and succeed goes away. Let's be honest, why should I work 60 hours a week, when my neighbor decides, he doesn't need to work, and he has the same things I do. Heck to be honest, a lot of people will stop working. Why work when I can get everything for free and live the same as everyone else.

As you can see equality doesn't work. It destroys one will, to succeed and there's no dignity or respect to gain by working. You can't have half the country working and the other half not working and sustain a good economy or environment, it leads to a lot of issues.

As you can see, the American dream is gone because of equality. Well, the new American dream is equality anyhow, might as well get used to it. There's plenty of people jumping on board with this theory. If it's ever implemented, it will be the end of our economy as we know it.

You might have the attitude that this won't affect me. Well maybe you will check out, before this happens. But if you care about your kids or grandkids future, you might want to think about what you're leaving them.

Our only way out of this is for the American people to change our attitude on how much money we are spending and racking up in debt. It will have to be paid off at some point. If we don't get a hold of it, the future will be interesting.

To sum up the last few chapters, I want you to remember one thing. Their plan is to take everything you have and control every aspect of your life. They are working on dismantling the constitution to make this happen.

Once the Constitution is dismantled, they will create laws to make this happen. Remember it's about them having everything and you having nothing. There's obviously a lot of wealth for them to gain, or they wouldn't be so adamant about it.

Work Until You Die

If you read the last two chapters, that's great. This chapter will tie into those because they all go hand in hand.

The retirement age has already changed a few times in the united states. There are several reasons for that. People are living longer. There aren't enough workers paying into the system to support social security,

Americas Future Paying Higher Taxes

Medicaid, and Medicare accounts. There's not enough money in the accounts. At least these are the excuses we hear.

The one thing you will notice as you read this book, is I don't have a problem telling the truth. I realize there's a lot of people that don't want to be blamed for the problems we have. The bottom line is we are all to blame because we allow it to happen. It's our country. It's time for all of us to look in the mirror and see how we are affecting our country. Or what we can do to help bring down the debt in our country.

Now, I want to say this before I go on. There's a lot of great people in America, there really is. We are some of the most generous people in the world. Most of us just live our normal lives and don't pay attention to what's happening in our country. The problem is our generosity is being taken advantage of and it's time we start paying attention before it's too late.

Let's talk about Social security first. Social security is a program that was set up for you to retire. While you work, you pay into social security, so when you retire, you can get a check to help pay your bills.

For years we've heard that the social security account is almost tapped out. That there's not enough money in the account for future generations. Do you think it's tapped out because we have too many retired people getting benefits? Do you think it because it's been mishandled? Do you think it's because a lot of people are taking advantage of the system?

Well, the answer is most likely all of them. But once

again, it would be in better shape if it weren't for the people that are taking advantage of the system. There you go, I bet someone is yelling and screaming at me right now, because I blamed us, As I've stated before, the truth hurts. I will make my point.

I'm going to tell you a card story. I like playing cards. I go to the casino periodically and I like to play cards. We have 8 people sitting at the table and coming across the room is a man pushing a lady in a wheelchair. As we see her coming, we all stand up and rearrange our chairs so she can be seated at our table in her wheelchair.

Like I said most of us are great people, there's a person in a wheelchair, make accommodations, it's only the polite thing to do. I wouldn't want to be bound to a wheelchair. I generally feel bad for anyone in a wheelchair. I wouldn't want to live that way.

After about an hour of playing, we are all having fun laughing, drinking and she's included, she's having just as much fun as anybody. She then says, I need to go to the bathroom. A couple of people say do you need help, she replies no.

She stands up and with back of her legs, shoves the wheelchair backwards, turns around and walks out of the room. Everybody goes dead quiet.

As she's walking across the room, we are all staring at her. She does not have hitch in her step. You can clearly tell she is walking perfectly normal. After 10 seconds of quietness. Here it comes, the rest of the players erupt.

Americas Future Paying Higher Taxes

What in the hell is that all about, I felt bad for her and she just walks out of here normal, like nothing's wrong? I'm willing to bet she's sucking off the system with her fake stuff. Not a wonder why our taxes are so high, etc. etc. etc. You got the point.

Now as I stated before, I don't think anyone has a problem helping someone that needs it. But clearly, we have a lot of people that are taking advantage of the rest of us. We are allowing this to happen.

If you read the last few chapters, you can see how all this ties together. Well Social security, Medicaid and Medicare are no different. As these accounts run out of money, the retirement age is going to go up. This will have to happen to keep bringing money into the system. Eventually the retirement age will be so high, that people will work until they die.

Now I'm about done talking about money, I think you get a vision of what the future looks like. But like I've done throughout this book, is tie things together. If you remember, I used Covid-19 as my reference when I was talking about higher taxes.

Remember I said it may be a bad example to use, but now you're going to find out why I used it. All the topics I talked about to this point, have already been in play for many years. They've had an agenda or plan to make all this happen already. Way before Covid-19 hit.

With any plan or agenda, you need an excuse. Covid-19 is going to be their excuse. The next thing you're going to hear is, we need to raise taxes. Covid-19. We need to cut benefits, Covid-19 etc. etc. You got the point.

Now don't get me wrong it didn't help us, but like I stated before, we already had a huge deficit before covid-19 showed up and a plan was already in place.

Now I always try to back up my point with some info. There was a certain person who made the statement that Covid-19 was a godsend. This statement was made almost immediately upon the arrival of Covid-19 in America. The problem is, he wasn't the only one that believed in this. They grabbed onto it and have been using covid-19 as an excuse for everything. They will continue to use it in the future for their agenda.

As far as I can see the United States is recovering. The national unemployment rate is 6.2% as of February 2021. This tells me the economy has recovered, people are going back to work. The highest unemployment during Covid-19 was in Michigan it was 23.6%. There unemployment rate is at 5.2%. Looks like Americas going back to work. So, there's no reason to keep using Covid-19 as an excuse, but they will.

But no matter how great we rebound, and the economy gets back too normal. Just remember you're going to hear covid-19 used a lot in the future. It will be used for higher taxes, lower benefits, whatever agenda they need it for.

Remember one thing, in order to execute a plan, you need an excuse. They are going to use Covid-19 for it. Don't be sympathetic towards them, that's what they want. Is to play off your emotions, so they can do what they want.

Americas Future Paying Higher Taxes

Let me prove a point. Most of America is ignoring what the Government is telling them about Covid-19. It's been over a year and most of us have went back to our normal lives because the science says we can.

Yet the Government continues to try to instill fear in the people. Demanding that businesses still stay closed, schools not to open. Kids who have a 1 percent chance of catching Covid-19 still must wear masks, which create other health concerns.

At the time I'm writing this, over half the population has been vaccinated. Yet they are still pushing their agenda. That's because they have a long-term plan, and it involves using Covid-19 to the nth degree. Luckily, some people aren't buying into it.

No Jobs & Poverty

I know we discussed taxes in the previous chapters. I asked the question. If you raise taxes on everyone making over 400 thousand a year and on companies, does it affect you. The answer is, yes it does.

When you raise taxes on anybody in the United States. It creates a trickledown effect. When you raise taxes on people or companies making over $400,000 a year. To recuperate the extra money that they're paying in taxes. They will either raise prices on their products, or layoff people? Either way, it trickles down.

When you raise taxes on big companies, they're lay people off or pass that expense down to you. So, in the long run, you're paying more for everything you buy.

Billy Grinslott

They're going to get it from you, by raising their prices

Not to mention, that some companies will move out of the country. Because they can get a better tax break. Which will cause more unemployment. It will also affect wages, you will be paid less, so they can recuperate the cost.

Now that we realize there's a trickledown effect on whatever happens to the economy. As taxes are raised on everyone, companies will decide to move out of the country to lessen their tax burden and expenses.

This means less jobs for the American people. The unemployment rate will go up because there will be fewer jobs. As more people are laid off, our economy will surely have problems.

Companies can afford to move out of the country, and they will, they've done it before because of tax liabilities. The problem is you can't move, so you're stuck here to deal with the aftermath.

The poverty rate in the United states has been increasing over the past several years. More people are relying on help for all items, especially food. America has seen an influx of people over the past several years, visiting food shelves and looking for assistance.

As the unemployment rate rises because companies have left the United States. The amount of people living in poverty will increase. This will send the economy into a downward spiral and will have drastic effects.

The more people on unemployment, means everyone must pay for them. Which means more taxes need to be collected? As you can see, things slowly

Americas Future Paying Higher Taxes

compound and get worse over time.

Because taxes must be raised, this will put a burden on the rest of the companies that are still in America. They will have to raise their prices to recuperate their loss.

The issue with this is, since everyone is paying higher taxes and you don't have much or any money to spend, you can't buy their products. The problem is now compounded for companies. High expenses and no money coming in from sales.

Guess what, they must cut costs. This means laying off people or shutting down. That's right I said it, many companies will not survive the burden that will be put on them and they will have to shut down.

Remember this one fact. Using taxes to create jobs, doesn't work. When you borrow money to create jobs, eventually the money runs out. Then you must borrow more money, the deficit goes up, more taxes need to be collected to pay that debt.

I don't care if it's the new green deal they're selling you or how they're promising new jobs. If you borrow money, the money will eventually run out and you will have to borrow more. This raises our debt and taxes will have to be raised to pay it back.

You can't use tax dollars to create jobs. It has bad consequences all the way around. When the money does run out and you can't borrow any more. People will be laid off.

By now, you get the point. There will be high unemployment and many more people living in poverty. This will have a detrimental effect on society. It will not be an enjoyable place to live for everyone.

The only way from keeping this from happening in the future, is for everyone to stop running up the deficit so high. If we don't change our habits and control our spending, future America will not be an enjoyable place to live.

Let's talk about being sold a bill of goods. The green new deal is one of these where you're not being told the truth. Who do you think is going to benefit from the green new deal? Do you think it's America's people?

They are promising good paying jobs to Americans. But those jobs come at a cost. Because they want to borrow the money from you to make it happen. Anyone with any business sense knows you can't borrow money to create jobs. Eventually it must be paid back.

Do you think the Governments going to pay it back? No, you are through taxation. When the money runs out, they will borrow more, that means higher taxes for you.

On top of that, the when the money does run out and the taxpayers get tired of flipping the bill. There will be a lot of people laid off. Say hello unemployment.

I asked the question of who is going to benefit from the green new deal. The politicians who own part of the companies that are going to be subsidized to do this work. The politicians that are getting kickbacks from companies doing the work. The companies that are doing the work.

Think of it this way. They don't do anything unless

Americas Future Paying Higher Taxes

it benefits them. How do you think some politicians get so rich? They use your tax dollars too subsidize their agenda.

Let's look at it from a different perspective. If the green new deal is so lucrative and there's money to be made, then why aren't companies coming forward to take on the challenge. Why should they when they can get subsidized and use the taxpayers and have no risk.

Speaking of being subsidized, do you know that we send money to other countries for the green new deal. That we're paying other countries for the Paris climate accord, to go green and they're not doing it. But they're more than happy to take our money.

The whole point behind this is you're being sold a bill of goods. A lot of people are going to get wealthy off the American people. You will pay for it with higher taxes and when they can't us your money anymore. You will be laid off. The green new deal will be a cost every taxpayer.

Voting Rights

One of the ways that Americans have been able to control how our country is run, is by voting. People love to vote because it gives them a chance to voice their opinion. It makes us feel good that we're involved on deciding on who will run our country.

The problem is there are people and organizations that want to change how we vote. Not only are they trying to change voting laws. They are trying to change who can vote.

In the 2020 Presidential election, there were many rule changes that surely affected the outcome of the vote. Mail in ballots allowed more people to vote. One of the issues with this is how do you know who is sending in the ballot with no way to verify it. It's been stated that this action led to some cheating. I'm not here to say it happened or didn't happen, but it does leave the possibility open.

There was also a lot of suppression going on. People didn't get the correct information needed to help them inform a good decision. This surely affected the outcome of the vote.

Some people and organizations want to do away with voter verification. As far as I can remember, we always had to show some proof of verification when voting. This allowed the legal citizens of the United States the chance to vote.

As far as I can tell, you need an ID for just about anything you do. So why should voting be any different. Here's why, Illegal aliens may not have ID's. They want everyone to vote because they feel that it benefits them.

Now they want to do away with voter registration and voter verification. What this means is anyone standing on American soil can vote. I don't think it's fair to the rest of us, that someone who does not have residency here should be able to vote. They shouldn't be able to decide how our country is run and who will be running it, when they don't have a vested interest in it.

Giving everyone citizenship just so they can vote is

Americas Future Paying Higher Taxes

not a good option either. I would think that we would want people entering our country, to believe in what our country stands for, support our beliefs and our constitution. It doesn't appear that certain people care about that. Everything is good if they can get a vote.

What this does is, take away your vote, it suppresses it. So, your vote no longer counts. Because you've been out voted by people who don't have a vested interest in or aren't citizens of the United States.

Giving up your right to vote is one of the last things, I would think, you would want to do. I personally thought it was important for most people to keep that right.

The future of federal election voting will look like this. Your vote will no longer count. Without voter Identification or verification, people will be bussed into this country to vote. They will come from all directions and it will happen.

They will pile across the borders to make sure whoever is elected benefits them. People will fly in and vote, then go back home. Trust me theirs some people and organizations that are going to support it. Just so they get the person they want in office.

Now that statement right there should give you some concern about protecting the integrity of the voting laws in the United states. But let's go on to the next point.

State elections will no longer be fair. Because if you don't have to prove state residency or voter verification, people will pile across the state line and vote in your election. That's right, you will have people from other states deciding who your elected officials are. Imagine if half of California showed up in your state election.

This is what your future looks like for voting if we don't stand up and protect voter registration and verification. Once this gone, we will have other countries deciding who our federal elected officials are.

Not to mention, you will have people who aren't residents or citizens of the United States choosing who your next elected officials are. They want to do away with your rights so illegal aliens can choose your next elected officials.

Of course, after we allow this to happen, their next step will be to eliminate voting all together. Then the elite and hierarchy will choose who will run the country. Trust me they will choose someone who benefits them and not the people.

If you don't think this is how they want it, you're sadly mistaken. The elite and hierarchy in this country really don't care about what you want. They want to run the country how they see fit.

As I'm writing this, the top companies in the US are having a meeting about how they want the voting rights set up. Want to know who's in charge of your country, it's not the people.

Remember this one thing from this book if you can, Politicians are bought and paid for. Now you know who owns them.

I'm not sure when Americans went soft. It seems that no one cares about protecting our country

Americas Future Paying Higher Taxes

anymore. We just allow everyone to walk all over us, while our rights and heritage are disappearing, and our country is falling apart in all aspects.

I've got a great idea and I'm just kidding when I say this. I'm going to vote like 30 or more times. If I don't have to prove who I am or where I'm from. I will just run from place to place and vote as many times as I can. That should make for a fair election, hay.

Better yet, wait till they bus in ten thousand people into your area, and they vote as many times as they can. You got the point.

If we don't stand up and protect our voting rights and put an end to these personal agendas and nonsense, you won't have a voice anymore.

Climate Change

If you believe in climate change or global warming good for you. For those of you who don't believe in it, I will try to give a simple perspective on why it's real.

The earth has a real cool deign to it. The trees and plants are designed to take in bad stuff like carbon dioxide, through a process called photosynthesis. To do this, their leaves pull in carbon dioxide and water through tiny pores. During that process, the tree releases 02, which is oxygen, from the leaves.

So, to make that last statement simple, trees and plants take in bad stuff from the atmosphere and convert it over to oxygen, they are basically a filter for our atmosphere, they clean it up and release oxygen that we need to breathe and survive.

Who do you think is responsible for all the emissions that are released in our atmosphere? This will be interesting can't wait till someone flies off the handle here and starts yelling at me. Guess who's responsible, that's right, all of us. Now I know some people are saying I'm wrong, it's not my fault, well it is.

Some people like to blame big companies for all the pollution, like power plants and refineries. The issue with this is, these companies have been put on strict pollution controls and emit little pollution compared to other things.

Did you know that all the cars driving around, put out way more emissions than companies do? Think about that next time you are driving. Did you know that lawnmowers put out a lot of emissions? Your house heater, etc. You got the point. You see, you are contributing to the issue.

Now how many people like to live in houses. Raise your hand. Well now that we know the trees are meant to clean up the atmosphere and supply oxygen. For every tree we chop down we are taking away mother nature's way of cleaning up the atmosphere. Look at your house and ask yourself how many trees were needed to build it. You might want to think about planting some trees.

To sum this, up. As the population grows more cars are driven, we pollute more. As we build more houses or use wood for other purposes, trees are taken away

Americas Future Paying Higher Taxes

and we reduce mother nature's way of supplying oxygen. Now don't get me wrong, there's more causes, but this just one simple way to look at it.

How does that create global warming or climate change? There's a tipping point. When we are emitting more pollution than the environment can clean up, the atmosphere fills up with gasses and creates a greenhouse effect. As the sun shines through the atmosphere, it heats up these gasses. This creates a warming of our atmosphere. The warming of the atmosphere effects everything, including the weather.

To sum all this up. We can't keep destroying the planet and not think that there's consequences to pay. The worst enemy for this planet is humans. We can't keep hacking away at the planets resources and expect nothing to happen. There's a tipping point.

The normal oxygen level is around 21%. How much do you think the oxygen level has to drop before it affects you? Do you think the oxygen level is the same everywhere on earth? The answer is No. Try climbing Mount Everest up into what they call the death zone. This is a point in elevation where the Oxygen is low enough to kill a person. Mountain climbers must take oxygen with them to make it to the top or they will die.

Back to answering the first question. The oxygen level only needs to drop a couple percent and it will start to have a diverse effect on you. Death will eventually happen as your body shuts down.

The next time you walk out of your house and take a whiff of that fresh air, see how many trees are around, if you don't see any, plant some. Eventually there won't be enough trees to overcome the pollution and you won't have any air to breathe.

How do we get out of this? We stop polluting, so mother nature can catch up. This means you can't drive any more, just kidding. The EPA has already worked with companies on reducing emissions. They have gone down significantly.

The other option is going green, solar, wind and water energy. This is already in the works but doesn't solve everything. One of the problems you have with going green is, all the countries must do it. If all the countries don't do it, it doesn't change anything.

Like I stated in the last chapter, we are subsidizing other countries to go green, and they aren't doing it. If everyone doesn't get on board, it will do no good.

If we don't do something, eventually the planet will protect itself. When it does it will wipe out the population and start over. It's done it before; it will do it again. Oh, don't worry, some people will survive, in some remote area where's there's enough oxygen. But most of us will die from not having enough oxygen to breathe.

Bottom line is we need to stop hacking down the trees that remove carbon dioxide, so they can continue to remove more of the greenhouse gasses from our atmosphere. We need to lower our emissions and plant more trees. It's the only way out of this.

Pay attention to mother nature, the weather is getting more violent. Tornadoes are happening earlier in the year. Thunderstorms are becoming more violent, dumping torrential rains. Snowstorms are affecting areas, that they normally don't. Hurricanes are stronger and more violent. All due to global warming.

If you don't think this will affect you, because you will be checking out before it happens, think of who you're leaving behind.

Immigration

Now I realize that most of us don't have a problem with immigrants coming to America. I think we all agree that if it's done right, we don't have a problem with it. I think most Americans don't mind diversity.

There's plusses and minuses of immigrants coming into our country. One of the plusses is we get to know people with different backgrounds, experiences, and cultures. I've personally worked with people from all different countries and have enjoyed getting to know them.

One of the people I've been fortunate to get to know over the last 30 years, came from Sweden. He came to America to go to college, applied for his citizenship and got it. We started working together 30 years ago and he taught me a lot. His degree is in chemical engineering.

Our job requires that we know some chemistry. I personally didn't have a clue about chemistry. He took under his wing and taught me what I needed to know. Without him, I wouldn't have succeeded the way I did.

What I'm trying to say is, there's some great people out there. I've had the pleasure to meet many people from different countries and have enjoyed it. My personal experience is great, but I know it's not like that for everyone.

There's a lot of plusses to immigration, there are also some minuses. As I stated before, I don't think anyone has an issue if it's done the right way. When it's done the right way, we can control our population and budget. So, our economy isn't ruined because of it. Here comes that part where I'm going to be honest, oh boy.

When people sneak into the united states, it puts a huge burden on our economy. We now must find a way to feed, clothe and house these individuals. This puts everyone in a spot where they need to pay more in taxes. It increases our population and there are downsides to that. This doesn't bother me as much as the next points.

When you come over to our country, obviously you did it because you didn't like your country. But you come over illegally and then you try to tell us that we can't pray to the God we believe in. That our religion needs to end because it doesn't match your religion or beliefs. Our churches need to be shut down. That's not right.

I think, we can both still pray to our gods and get along. We can both have different religions and faith and still get along. The important thing is it doesn't matter what god you pray too if you have faith. But when you try to impose beliefs upon us and tell us we

Americas Future Paying Higher Taxes

need to end our religion, because you don't agree with it, that's not right.

The American flag and constitution. Plenty of people in the united states have given their blood, sweat and tears to defend the American flag and constitution. These people are of all creeds, races, and religion. They have stood together for many years to protect our freedom. Not to mention that our military members from all walks of life. Have stood next to each other, fought next each other, and died to defend our freedom.

When you come over here and take our American flag down and burn it, you just irritated a lot of people. I'm not sure what gives you the right to come over here and dishonor our country. You came over because you wanted freedom. The American people fought to give you that opportunity and then you disgrace us by burning our flag.

You want to try and tell us that we must live the way you lived. Obviously, that wasn't good for you, because you left your country You come over here and try to destroy our country, our constitution. If we are not good enough for you, go back home.

I'm not sure what gives you a right to come over to our country and tell us that we need to change. That we need to forget about our heritage, forefathers and what our country stands for. You have no right to impose your countries views upon our country. Your country wasn't working for you and you left. Why would we want our country to run like that?

I want everyone to know that not all immigrants are

to blame for these actions. There's plenty of great people from other countries that live in America and are great citizens. The issue we have is like always, there's a certain group out there that are causing problems. They need to be stopped, so the rest of us can live in peace. Round them up and send them packing if they don't want to accept our way of life.

So, for all the great immigrants and the American people, our kindness is being taken advantage of. We need to voice our opinions to our leaders and have them get control of this, so we can live happy lives.

One last note. This book was published in 2021 and the influx of people that are piling across our border needs to stop. We need to let them know that we don't agree to this, just because they have a personal agenda, doesn't make it right. We are the ones that must pay the tab.

Let's look at some ill effects of letting illegal immigrants uncontrolled into America. We already discussed the fact that they come over and try to change our way of life. Some of them disgrace our country, what it stands for and try to force their ideals on us.

Illegal immigrants put a huge strain on our economy. We must pay to feed, clothe, and house these individuals. Not to mention we must pay for their education. One more reason we must pay more in taxes.

Last, we don't know who they are, some of these illegal immigrants could be criminals, drug dealers, or terrorists. This is bad for all of us. Our neighborhoods will less safe. Society is less safe; you got the idea,

Americas Future Paying Higher Taxes

there's some really bad stuff that happens by not controlling our borders.

Overpopulation

I Realize that most people don't think that the United States will become overpopulated. But every country faces overpopulation at some point. The United States is included in this and will face this in the future.

There's a lot of things that lead to overpopulation. One is people are living longer. Since people are living longer and kids are still being born, this raises the total population. The other is immigration, other people coming to our country.

Immigration is fine if you control it. Every year many people enter our country uncontrolled, nobody really knows how many. In 2021 we had a mass amount of people enter our country. This leads to a higher population and puts a strain on our resources.

I realize that when you look at America, we still have a lot of vast open lands and you think that the united states could never be overpopulated.

Overpopulation doesn't necessarily mean that you have a person standing in every square foot of the country. Overpopulation occurs when you have too many people and not enough food to feed them or resources to take care of them.

It doesn't matter how much open land you have. If

you can't raise enough livestock or grow enough crops to feed the amount of people you have. It means that the country is overpopulated.

Every country faces a risk of overpopulation, the United states is no different. At some point in the future, we will face this. The next chapter will cover the effects of overpopulation in more depth.

Starvation, Food Shortages

I realize, Americans are used to the land of plenty. We are most likely the worst when it comes to food, we waste a lot of it. America typically has an abundance of food and we've gotten used to that. In the future, we will face a food shortage.

Every country faces a food shortage at some point. The main reason is overpopulation. As I stated in the last chapter, Overpopulation doesn't mean that you have a person standing in every square foot of the country. Overpopulation occurs when you have too many people and not enough food to feed them or resources to take care of them.

It doesn't matter how much open land you have. If you can't raise enough livestock or grow enough crops to feed the amount of people you have. It means that the country is overpopulated and faces a food shortage.

Let me give you an example of what we are seeing in America. As the population grows, every time you build a house or take up farmland for other reasons,

Americas Future Paying Higher Taxes

you reduce the amount of land you have, to grow food. As I stated in some of the other chapters, there's a trickledown effect.

As we take up more land, there's not only not enough food to feed us, but there's not enough to feed the livestock. Americans are used to eating both. When you can't feed the livestock, you can't raise new livestock and you can't keep the livestock you have, alive.

Let me ask you a question. How much beef do Americans consume every year? In 2019 America consumed 27.3 billion pounds of beef. That's just beef, it doesn't include all the other meat products and fish. I don't know how many cows it takes to get 27.3 billion pounds of beef, I bet it's a lot.

My point is as the population grows and you take up land, you eventually get to a tipping point. You have too many people and not enough food to feed us or livestock. Not to mention that as the population grows, you need more food and livestock. Farmers are already having issues in today's world with raising enough livestock to feed everyone.

Do you like to eat the creatures that come from the oceans and seas? It's been reported that we are already depleting the amount of seafood available. So, the problem has already started.

Every country faces this at some point. Let's look at some other countries and trust me many of us could not stomach what they eat. Some countries are so overpopulated, they do have a food shortage.

Billy Grinslott

If you're ever curious of what's eaten, do some searching. I will give you a hint. If it slithers, crawls, walks, flies, or breathes, they eat it. So, next time you see a worm or bug in your yard, think about that. Some countries think that's a delicacy. They cook it up and eat it.

Here's what happens when there's a food shortage. The first thing is the store shelves will be empty. Anyone that witnessed what happen during Covid-19 can attest to this. The store shelves were empty in a matter of days. The store shelves don't get restocked very quickly because suppliers can only handle so much demand or they don't have any left.

As people get hungry, they will find alternative ways to find food. If you live in the country, you will survive for a while. You can always shoot some squirrels or whatever. But if you live in the city, you're in trouble.

When people need food, they become desperate, and they will be knocking down your door to get it. That's right, when people get hungry, they will turn to theft and robbery to eat. They will do whatever they need to, to feed themselves, their family and to survive.

Now some people are thinking I'm nuts right about now. So, I will give you an example. When Covid-19 hit the United States and the stores were going empty, it took about a week and people were being robbed. People were being held up right in the grocery store parking lot. They would come out of the store with their groceries and get robbed.

As you can see, people become desperate when they

need food. Eventually that desperation will end up turning into total chaos. Everyone will do what they need to do, to get food and survive. Even if that includes drastic measures.

As I said before, every country faces food shortages. The United States will also face it in the future. With our population growing and many immigrants that are piling across the border, it may happen sooner than later.

Now you might be sitting there thinking this won't affect me. I will be off the planet before that happens. If you care about the people, you're leaving behind, then it's time to step up to the plate and I don't mean dinner plate.

Pandemics, Diseases & Viruses

If you witnessed COVID-19 and you think that the United States is done seeing pandemics, diseases, or viruses in the future, you're sadly mistaken. Our country has seen plenty of these outbreaks through its history and it will happen again.

The more overpopulated our country gets, it's likely we will see more of these outbreaks. Every species on this planet has diseases and susceptible to contracting new ones.

One risk we have is when people come from other countries. They may have diseases or viruses that we don't. Our military members must get vaccinated before they go to another country. But people coming into our country don't. This allows viruses to spread.

Whether you believe in getting vaccines or not, I think is a personal choice. There are some risks involved, on the other hand I understand it.

I think vaccines that have been used over a lengthy time are most likely fine. There's plenty of data to back them up. I have questions and doubts about new vaccines, especially if they're rushed to market.

I personally am not a pill popper. How many times do you find out years later that a pill that was used to treat someone, has bad side effects? For example, it causes cancer, kidney disease, liver disease or something else. You got the point.

Heck, stay awake late at night and listen to the drug ads. Listen to all the side effects from some drugs. Some pills have more side effects than the problem.

When it comes to new vaccines, I can see why some people may have concerns. Even with Covid-19 one of the vaccines has been put on hold due to problems. We don't know what the long-term effects are of these vaccines.

On the other hand, vaccines have done great wonders to keep America healthy. So, I think in the long run vaccines are good and should be taken. Once proven effective and knowing what the side effects are.

Here's why. Diseases and viruses that we've spent many years trying to eliminate through vaccines will come back and they will affect future generations. Everyone who decides not to get vaccinated, puts everyone else at risk.

Americas Future Paying Higher Taxes

People always have diseases and viruses, there are several viruses that are among us all the time. One of the most common is Influenza and pneumonia, the flu. It's been with us for a long time.

Viruses are hard to get rid of because they adapt and put off new strains. It's one reason why we can't eliminate the flu virus, it's constantly changing and adapting. Viruses can also adapt to the vaccine over time and become stronger.

Covid-19 has already branched off into different strains. Covid-19 will most likely turn out like the flu virus. We will be dealing with well into the future. All though, there's still a lot of debate on how Covid-19 originated, it doesn't matter because it may be here to stay.

We got lucky with the Covid-19 virus. Stop and take a deep breath, by now you should know, I'm going to make a point. I don't want to downplay what happened; it was bad for a lot of people. What I want to say is we got lucky that it wasn't one of those viruses that if you caught it you die. We got lucky that most people were able to fight off the virus and live.

Let me give you an example. The Spanish flu was much worse, it killed more than 50 million people in one year, that's right I said more than 50 million people. Covid-19 looks like an infant compared to the Spanish flu. If Covid-19 would have been anything like the Spanish flu, the mortality rate would have been much higher. So, we got lucky.

I realize that most people have this attitude, well if

a virus appears there's nothing to worry about. Our scientists will create a vaccine, and all is good. Well, that's not the way it works.

The virus hits first and then a vaccine is made, that's how it works. It took a little over a year for vaccines to come out for Covid-19. Can you imagine if Covid-19 were as deadly as the Spanish flu, what kind of havoc it would have reaped upon us.

You must take into consideration that a virus may hit that we can't find a cure or vaccine for. We have diseases and viruses in our world today, that we don't have cures for.

So, in the same amount of time, a little over a year. That's how long it took us to come up with a vaccination for Covid-19. The Spanish flu killed over 50 million people, in that same time frame. We were fortunate Covid-19 wasn't as deadly as the Spanish flu.

As you can see, we have experienced pandemics before and we will face another pandemic in the future, it's guaranteed. Eventually we will experience a virus that is way worse than anything we've ever seen. It's happened before and it will happen again.

Guns, Guns, Guns

Talking about guns can be a very controversial issue. Some people believe in having guns and others don't. Either way it's a topic that needs to be addressed. We have some real issues with guns that need our attention and guns are important to help protect society and need

Americas Future Paying Higher Taxes

to be protected.

We will cover both topics, gun control and protecting the Second Amendment. Hopefully, it will make sense of why we need better gun control, but also why we need to protect our gun rights and the ability to own a gun.

We must have a happy medium when it comes to both these issues. We will need guns in the future and the ability to protect ourselves. By the time you're done reading this book, you will see many reasons of why we want to protect our rights.

When I discuss topics or look at issues, I try to keep an open mind and look at all points of view. I'm an open-minded person and I believe that we should be able to discuss a topic and still have respect for each other by having different opinions.

During this chapter, I hope to give you a different look at guns, why we need some gun control and why they will be important in the future to protect your rights and way of life.

Let me tell you a little about myself before we get into this. I personally am a gun owner. I've been around guns all my life. My spouse, my kids and everyone else in our family have been around guns our whole life. We are outdoorsman and enjoy it. We are responsible gun owners like most people. I'm no different than you are. I'm an average American citizen.

I was taught to respect people. Don't get me wrong, I respect guns, but I respect people's lives more. I believe that every person has a right to live a good life and not have that taken from them by an unstable person with a gun. I believe that we should protect everyone, from this happening. Whether you are a gun owner or not.

This brings me to the first topic and that is gun violence. Before I get on with this, I want to say that my heart goes out to anyone who has lost someone due to gun violence. No one should ever have to go through that, our prayers and thoughts are with you.

We as a nation have a major crisis on our hands and that is gun violence, the gun violence in America needs to stop. The people of the United States and our elected officials need to come up with a solution and put an end to these senseless shootings.

There is no way that a family going out shopping, should have to worry about being shot, because some mentally unstable person got a hold of a gun. Kids should not have to go to school and worry about somebody coming into their classroom and shooting them. This shouldn't happen in America.

No one in America should have to worry about being shot at. We should be able to go on with our normal lives and not have the stress of worrying about this. Yet we have a few individuals and groups that seem to want to disrupt our lives. Whether you are a gun owner or not, I think we can all agree on this.

As a Gun owner, I believe, I have the right to own a gun. I also believe that a mother or child that was shot and killed has a right to live. They didn't deserve to die at the hands of some lunatic that got a hold of a gun.

Americas Future Paying Higher Taxes

They had a right to live and go on with their lives.

As you can see, this is a slippery slope. On one hand we need to protect our second amendment and our rights to gun ownership. On the other hand, we must try to figure out a way to protect everyone from these senseless shootings. What I do know is if we as a nation, don't do something about it, in the future it's going to get much worse.

Over 40,000 people died from gun violence last year in America. I think we all agree there is a need for gun control. But taking guns from good citizens isn't the answer.

Who's to blame for all the gun violence in America. Some people want to blame the gun owners, others want to blame on the guns, others want to blame it on the government. Let's look at all of these.

Let's start with gun owners. Most gun owners are respectful, law abiding citizens. The only reason they bought a gun, was to protect themselves and their families. They never use the gun unless they need it for self-defense.

Hunters and outdoorsman own a lot of guns, they are typically used for sport. Again, most of these gun owners are respectful law-abiding citizens. The bottom line is most gun owners aren't responsible for gun violence.

What about the gun, is it too blame? In my 50 years of being around guns, I have never seen or witnessed this. I have never seen a gun unlock the gun cabinet. Walk out of the gun cabinet. Grab some bullets and load itself. Then walk down the street and shoot someone.

If the day comes that I witness this, I will directly drop to my knees and start praying. Because Jesus Christ has returned, or I've been possessed. I hope its Jesus, I believe in him. My point is the gun is not capable of loading itself or shooting anyone. Have you heard the saying, don't shoot the messenger because it's not his fault? The same goes for a gun, it can't physically do it, so it can't be blamed.

What about blaming the Government? Like I said, I'm an open-minded person and I try to look at things from all different views. I can't directly blame the government for these shootings, they didn't buy the gun, hand it to someone and tell them to shoot someone. So, we can't directly blame them, but indirectly they may have a different agenda.

The real issue we have with gun violence is, we have a few individuals in our society that are unstable, mentally ill, that should not own a gun. Not to mention, that we have gangs and criminals carrying guns and threatening good people every day. So, why isn't the issue being dealt with. Why aren't the people who are in control of this country dealing with getting guns out of the hands of these unstable individuals and groups.

They have the means and power to create a task force to take out these gangs or create very stringent laws with way better background checks, to keep guns out of the hands of these unstable individuals and criminals. Yet it hasn't been done.

If you notice, most of these mass shootings are

Americas Future Paying Higher Taxes

done by unstable individuals or criminals with a criminal record. Yet they still manage to get a gun somehow. Doesn't make much sense why our laws aren't strict enough to keep this from happening.

I think most responsible gun owners would have no issue with stricter laws. We will still be able to pass a background check. So, we will be fine.

Every time we have a mass shooting, the firsts words you hear are, we need to take guns away, we need to ban guns, we need to confiscate guns. You don't hear that we need to address this and find a way to change laws and make it impossible for these few individuals to get guns. No, the first response is to leave the responsible gun owners defenseless. This might be part of their personal agenda.

Leaving society and responsible gun owners defenseless isn't a good plan and shouldn't even be considered. First, it leaves you vulnerable to attacks from every criminal. It takes away your means of protecting your house, your family or business. If you've ever pondered the idea that society would be better off without guns, you might want to rethink it.

Does taking guns away from the good hardworking, honest American people, solve the problem of gun violence. The answer is no. Thugs, thieves, criminals, drug dealers and gang members will still have guns.

If you doubt this fact, I will clear it up for you. Drugs are illegal, yet they have been pouring into our country for years. If drug dealers can get drugs into the country, cartels will bring in weapons. The criminals will find a way to get a gun.

What this means for you is, since you bought into the idea that society would be better off without guns, you're now defenseless against thugs, thieves, criminals, drug dealers and gang members. You will no longer be able to protect yourself and your family from violence. Not a winning situation.

Right now, we have an issue in the United States. The issue is criminals are not being held for gun charges, they're just being released back into the streets. I just watched a report where a gang member was arrested for his 5th time for carrying an illegal gun. He was released with no bail. This isn't good for society it puts everyone at risk.

Not to mention, that the people rioting in the streets are also released without any charges. I'm wondering at what time in our country did this get to be acceptable. We have individuals and organizations fighting to let people out of jail, to fulfill their own personal agenda. It's time for the rest of America to voice our opinion and put an end to this.

How about catch and release, nice plan. Catch criminals, set a court date for them, and let them go. This act puts our whole society at risk. I just want to know when criminals ended up with more rights than good law-abiding citizens. I can go to jail for jaywalking, but a criminal can murder someone and be set free.

Did you know that firearms are used in self-defense to protect a home, family, or business, from two to three million times a year? Did you know that over the

Americas Future Paying Higher Taxes

past two years women have bought more guns than anybody?

The reason I brought that up is because it shows that people want a way to protect themselves and their families from violence. The only way to do this is to stand up and protect the 2nd amendment.

The only way to stop gun violence is to go after the bad guys and take them out of the equation. Taking away the good citizens way to protect themselves does not solve the problem. The only way we can ensure we have this right, is to protect the 2nd amendment.

Consider one last fact. The only thing that keeps another country or our country from taking over, is a well-armed militia, that's you They know if they step foot on our soil, they will have every armed person to contend with. Therefore, everyone owning a gun helps keep our country safe from domestic and foreign entities.

Now you might laugh at this, but by the end of this book, you will see who will be coming after us and who will own this country and rule over you. It's just a matter of time, but it's going to happen.

There's plenty of organizations and people out there that want to take your guns. That's why we need to stand up for our rights, protect the 2nd Amendment.

If we don't find a way to help put an end to the gun violence we are seeing. They are going to use it to take your guns. There's people and organizations that have already put this plan into action. They're already working on it.

Now you might ask yourself why they want to take your guns. The answer is simple. Whether you realize it not, they have a plan to take over everyone's life and have you do whatever they say and what they want.

If you've heard the words socialism or communism, it's their plan. They want to control every aspect of your life, this includes financially, they want it all.

The only way they can do this is to leave you defenseless. Once they dismantle the constitution and take your guns away, you won't be able to resist the rest of their actions, because you are left defenseless.

They know that in order to push their full agenda of controlling every aspect of your life, they need to disarm you. So, you have no way to stand up for your rights or stop their agenda.

Once they disarm you. They will be able to take over every aspect of your life with ease because you can't stand up for yourself. As I stated, they're already working on this.

We have 380 million people in the US, it's a small percentage of people that are involved in gun violence. Did you notice that every time an incident of gun violence, a riot or protest occurs, it's headline news for weeks?

The reason for this is so they can try to persuade more people into thinking that we have a much larger issue, than it really is. The more people they can persuade, the easier it is to take guns away.

So, how do we keep them from taking guns. We need to voice our opinions and let them know, we don't

Americas Future Paying Higher Taxes

agree with their personal agenda of taking over the country. We need to protect the constitution and the 2nd amendment and stand up for gun ownership.

One last thing before we move on to the next chapter. As you read this book, you will want to keep in your mind your right to keep and bear arms. The future for the United States isn't looking good. Now I'm not a doom and gloom type of guy, but the writing is on the wall and we are set on a path to go through some hard times in America. You will want a gun in the future.

Race Riots, Wars Among us

Right now, in the United States we already have an issue with racial tension. It has gotten worse over the past several years. The division in our country has grown. Not due to the good American people, we have other forces inciting it.

I never understood it myself. I don't wake up in the morning with hatred toward someone else. I don't blame other people for my problems. I just go about my life like normal and it's the last thing that ever crosses my mind.

I believe that most Americans are the same. Most Americans are not racist. Most Americans are very generous and will give you the shirt off their back. Americans are one of largest groups of people that donate to just about every cause. Not only in America, but globally.

When there's a crisis in the United States, most Americans stand up and help. They help in multiple ways, monetarily and many show up in person. America has the largest number of people willing to volunteer.

Every time there's a crisis in America the people show up in numbers to help. Whether they are cleaning up, rebuilding, supplying food or water. They give their blood, sweat and tears to help. It doesn't matter what color, race, or religion the person is that they're helping, they show up. This action proves that most Americans are not racist and will help anyone that needs it.

The problem we have in America is, there's small groups of people and a few organizations that want to portray that we have a bigger issue with racism and it's not true. They want to portray that America itself is racist and that's far from the truth. They are trying to force feed it to everyone else for their own personal agendas.

It seems that there are certain groups of people and organizations that are prone to forcing racial tensions onto the rest of us. It seems that it's the only way they know how to deal with issues or to push their own personal agendas.

Let's talk about groups and organizations pushing their own personal agendas. When George Floyd died, I'm sure there was some people that were upset or affected by this. I don't want to take anything away from that or diminish that fact.

But there were groups and organizations that used

Americas Future Paying Higher Taxes

it as a tool to raise racial tensions in our country and pour fuel onto the fire for their own personal agendas. We had certain groups and organizations that invoked chaos and rioting in our streets.

They didn't care one bit about George Floyd or what happened to him. That's the truth. They just needed an excuse to push their own personal agenda and they used George Floyd for it. They were just waiting for an excuse and jumped into action.

The problem is these groups and organizations did a lot of damage to good neighborhoods. By invoking rioting, luting, and burning down many good hard working Americans things. They created chaos for all of us. These organizations and groups are still using it as their excuse to push their own personal agendas.

Before I move on. I want to say that I believe black lives do matter, I believe all lives matter. I think many people are aware that these groups and organizations used everyone else to push their own personal agendas and that's not fair to everyone else. They invoked chaos and that was not most people's agenda.

They also took away your right to protest peacefully, voice your concerns and be heard, that's not fair. I believe that people do have a right to protest peacefully when issues arrive. But, when you have groups and organizations inciting riots for their own personal agenda, it doesn't help anyone. Especially when they really don't care about what the real issue is. That's not fair for everyone else involved or who did care.

Billy Grinslott

I never understood why some people want to blame others for their issues. Many Americans have issues. They get up in the morning and look in the mirror and try to figure out a solution to the problem. They don't run around blaming someone else.

Running around all day blaming someone else or being agitated does no good. It turns you into a miserable person. Then you just start living a miserable life and make everyone around you miserable. Doesn't sound like much fun.

At the time I'm writing this we have 382 million people in the United states. We have a few thousand people and a few organizations that are causing issues. It's a small percentage compared to the total population.

As you can see, with such a large population, it's only a few people or organizations that are pushing their agenda. We don't have an overall problem with racism, not like they want us to believe. Most Americans are great people and don't care about race at all. There's not an issue with systemic racism like they want you to believe.

Here's the problem we face in America. The more we allow these groups and organizations to affect our opinions or beliefs, the more people will start believing it's true. The more people that are swayed into believing it's true, will create more racial tensions among everybody.

The more racial tensions that are created, will create more problems between all of us. The next thing

Americas Future Paying Higher Taxes

you know we will have a bigger problem than what really exists. This is not a good scenario and doesn't need to happen. It will not be good for any of us and will lead to major problems in the future.

What we need to do is turn off and ignore all the negative energy that is being force fed to us, even by our own government. Their only mission is to turn all of us against each other, so they can say, see we do have a problem. Then they will use it for their own personal agenda. We must find a way to put an end to this.

It's time that America comes together and stop these people that are trying to divide us. The division that they're creating is not good for America and will only lead to more racial tensions. Their plan to tear everyone apart for their own personal agendas, needs to stop.

It's time for us to stand up and stop with the social media garbage. Turn off the news sources that are portraying America as a systemically racist country, cause it's not true. Time for us to tell our government to stop with their personal agenda of tearing America apart, so they can rebuild it.

If we don't learn to tune out all the negative forces, the future of the United states will not be a genuinely nice place to live. We will all be pitted against each other and we will have racial wars amongst our own people. I think most of us don't want to see that happen. It's time we start focusing on positive energy and focus on making America a great place to live, for everyone.

Lastly, you are being used and manipulated for others personal agendas. America doesn't have a systemic racism problem. Americans are some of the greatest people on this planet. Please don't be fooled by their personal agendas.

Cops or no Cops. Defunding the Police

Well, the issue of whether we should have police or not, is becoming a big topic in America. It's creating a lot of controversy. Many people call this defunding the police or dismantling the police altogether. I'm positive that not having police, will be bad for society.

I'm not sure where most of the population benefits from not having police. Yet we have certain people and organizations pushing to get rid of police. There main goal is to make the police look like the bad guys and in 99% of the cases, it's not true. They have their own personal agendas; we will get to that later.

The problem you have is every time there's a police shooting in America, you don't get all the facts. There's many people and organizations out there that are exploiting these shootings for their own personal agenda. They don't care one bit about the individual who was shot, all they care about is their agenda. They are using Americans as a pawn in their chess game.

Now, as usual, I like to give examples. On 4/12/21 a kid by the name of Daunte Wright was shot and killed during a traffic stop. I want you to watch the video of this incident. Just type in Daunte Wright Brooklyn

Americas Future Paying Higher Taxes

Center MN Body Cam. It will show everything that happens, but I will run through the course of events and give you a real look.

The kid is pulled over for having expired tabs on his vehicle, legitimate reason. Everything starts out as a normal traffic stop. What you don't know, but the cops do know, is he has warrant out for his arrest. The warrant is for multiple weapon charges.

It looks like a normal traffic stop. The cops approach the car in a normal manner and ask the kid to get out of the car. The kid complies and all is going well. At some point during the time that the officer is trying to put handcuffs on the kid, he decides, he doesn't want to comply anymore.

He wrestles himself away from the cop and jumps back in his car in an attempt, to flee. This is where the chaos starts. He is accidently shot by an officer who thought she had her taser, instead of her firearm. The outcome is a tragedy, I don't want to take anything away from that, but I will make my point.

If the kid would have complied, the shooting would have never happened. His actions made the rest of this scenario play out in a bad way. He put everyone in a bad spot, his actions caused this to happen. If he would have just complied, he would still be alive. That's a fact.

Now the other fact is this. He had a warrant out for his arrest. This means that he decided not to go to court and face whatever he was charged for. He made the decision to avoid dealing with it. Then when the cops do catch up to him and it's time to deal with it, he decides once again to flee the scene.

If he would have dealt with it right away, no one would have been put in this spot. Yet you want to blame the cops, because he didn't take care of it when he should have. There must be some ownership here.

Let's talk about Makhia Bryant. She is a black girl that was shot by a cop, while she was trying to stab another girl. Almost Immediately some people and organizations start yelling racism.

There is nothing in either one of theses videos that indicates any racism at all. When you watch the Makhia Bryant video, make sure you watch both the cop cam and the neighbors garage video.

The cop has literally seconds to react to a chaotic scene. She tries to stab another girl and she is going to stab the girl in pink and the cop makes the right decision to defend that girl's life.

I don't think that in the few seconds this cop had to react to a girl on a rampage trying to stab other people, that race even entered his mind. He reacted to the situation and that's all. Not a racist issue.

It's tough being honest isn't it. In both these cases, the perpetrator determines the outcome. If you comply, you don't get shot. If you own up to and face what you need too and take care of your business, you don't get shot. If you don't run around with a knife and try to stab someone you live.

Now, I was going to try to stay away from talking about George Floyd, but I must address it. Why, because it sparked one of the biggest uproars in our

Americas Future Paying Higher Taxes

country. I think we all agree that the way that George died on that day was not right. It was uncalled for, I'm with everyone on that. I just want everyone to understand that.

But here's where I think a lot of people have an issue. George Floyd was not a role model citizen. He had a rap sheet the length of his arm. Yet everyone is trying to portray him as a great citizen, pillar of the community.

Role model citizens don't commit crimes against other people. They surely don't threaten people's lives with a gun. On the day of his incident, he was committing another crime. If he was a role model citizen like the rest of us, he would have been at home baking cookies, not drugs.

My point is, none of this happens if George Floyd is a role model citizen. His actions of being a career criminal and doing another crime, is what causes all this to happen. The cops would have had no reason to be there. His criminal activities brought all this on. The result was tragic, but he created it by being a criminal.

The truth hurts don't it. When you get right to the bottom of it, his way of life of being a criminal and his actions caused all of it. If he would have ran his life like a role model citizen, he wouldn't have put anyone in that situation.

Some of society needs a reality check. The very minute that you take a criminal and you turn him into a national hero. We have some real issues in America that need to be addressed. If you think George Floyd is a hero, you've got some rethinking to do. A real hero is a cop that puts his life on the line to protect society from criminals.

I realize that a lot of Americans are smart enough to dig into the facts, before they make a rash decision and start blaming the cops. But we have some people that just want to fly off the handle, start yelling, screaming, and acting out right away. Without knowing all the facts.

Try educating yourself first before flying off the handle. I think you will discover that the people that the cops are trying to get off our streets, are not good for our society. We have a lot of great people in our society and most of us just want to live a peaceful life. We don't want criminals running our streets and controlling our neighborhoods.

By the way, stop yelling racism every time one of these shootings happen. Get the facts, there's more white people killed during police shootings than blacks. It's more than double. So, it's not a race issue and many cops are not racist. We don't have a systemic race issue like certain people and organizations want you to believe.

There's more black-on-black shootings than any other shootings, but nobody's complaining about that. Yet every time a cop shoots a black person who is most likely a criminal or committing a crime, it becomes a big deal. Most shootings in black neighborhoods are done by black people and there's no issue here. Nobody wants to talk about that. 95% of blacks killed are killed

Americas Future Paying Higher Taxes

by black people.

Doesn't make sense. It appears to me you might want more cops in your neighborhood to help deal with this, so you can live in peace. No one is talking about what's happening in your neighborhood, why not.

Why aren't we addressing the real issues. The crime in your community. We're not dealing with the real issue, instead we're trying to blame everyone else. When the real issue is in your own community.

20 blacks are killed every day in this country by the violence happening in their own neighborhoods, by their own people. Not one word is mentioned or are the real issues being dealt with. Everyone is ignoring the real issue and trying to use the race card to push their own personal agendas.

We need to deal with the real issues, so you can have a nice neighborhood to live in. Stop the government and other organizations from using blacks, black crime or police shootings for their own personal agenda. Get them to deal with the real issue and that is making your community a better place to live.

Let me bring up one more point and I want you to think about this. Did you know that during a criminal's career, at some point he will escalate to extremely bad violence? This means that at some point he's going to hurt or kill someone.

I hope it's not you, your family or kids that experience this. Because you made the decision to defund or dismantle the police. Someone must remove the criminals before this happens. If you defund or dismantle the police, many people will experience the wrath of criminals.

Police reform. I'm sure that police can learn or use new techniques. But what's being portrayed to America is some people don't want cops to carry guns. So, you're trying to tell us that it's ok for criminals to carry guns, but cops should not. So, your good with criminals running around and shooting up your neighborhood. When you call a cop to respond, that doesn't have a gun, how's that going to work out for you.

You're also telling us that a criminal has a right to protect his life, but a cop doesn't. Let's think about this. Most cops are hardworking average American citizens, that took a vow to protect society from thugs, thieves, and criminals. You're saying that a cop's life is worth less than a criminal's life. You want cops to get shot and killed with no way to defend themselves from the criminals that they're trying to protect you from. This makes no sense at all.

I've got a plan, check this out. I say we hire way more cops, give them as many guns as they need. Get the military involved and they go out and round up every criminal in America. Ship them to a deserted island somewhere. Then the rest of us can live in peace without all this chaos.

Now let me ask you a question. Do you think cops get up in the morning and say, I'm going to go out and shoot someone Today? Do you think they get up with the attitude they want to go out and confront, thugs, thieves, and criminals every day? Do you think they

Americas Future Paying Higher Taxes

enjoy dealing with criminals?

I doubt it, most cops are average citizens. They would love nothing more than to go to work and have a nice peaceful quite day like the rest of us at our jobs. But every society breeds criminals. Someone must deal with the criminals. If you want to do it yourself, then defund or dismantle the police and you will get your chance.

Defunding or getting rid of the police is the worst thing you could do for society; it puts everyone at risk. The thugs, thieves and criminals will own your neighborhood. They will be knocking down your door to get what you have. They will own you and take whatever dignity you have left.

You might want to buy a gun because you will have to defend yourself. You could call 911, but nobody's there, so you are left to defend yourself and your family. You just signed up to be cop by defunding the police.

Now that you have the attitude that defunding the police was a great thing, let me give you some information on what police officers must face. It is April 14th of 2021 and this year over 100 cops have been shot and died while on duty. That's about 1 cop a day getting shot and dying. How would you like to go to work and deal with that? Like I said, defund the police and you will get the opportunity.

The odds of you experiencing a criminal at your door will increase drastically, because the only thing keeping the criminals from knocking your door down right now is the police. Get rid of the police and you will get an opportunity to have criminals knocking down your door. I'm not sure about you, but I would rather have a cop knocking on my door, not a criminal.

If you defund police or dismantle the police, the criminals will be running society. It will be total chaos. You will not be able to go anywhere because you will be confronted by thugs, thieves, and criminals. The streets and neighborhoods will not be safe. Your kids will not be able to go to school because the gang members will rule them. Your kids will not be able to go outside because gangs will be controlling every neighborhood.

There will be many innocent people getting attacked and shot, because that's how gang members deal with things. The United States will revert to the wild, wild west. Everyone will be carrying a gun and it will look like a shootout at the ok corral.

Bottom line is, it will not be safe to go anywhere or do anything. By defunding or dismantling cops, you just signed away your right to be free. You'll no longer have the freedom to go anywhere or doing anything.

To live in a society where we can have freedom, we must have laws. The laws must be enforced, and someone must enforce them. Without laws, society turns into total chaos. You can't live in a society without laws. The minute you remove laws, society is taken over by thugs, thieves, and criminals.

By now there's a couple things running through your mind while you're reading this. Because I'm so adamant about not defunding the police. You're thinking I'm a cop, the answer is no. I just know what's

Americas Future Paying Higher Taxes

going to happen to society if you have no police. The outcome is detrimental for all of us and I'm not alone in my decision not to defund police.

85% of Americans that were polled, said they don't want the police to be defunded. The poll showed they want more police. A poll that was done among black citizens showed that 80% didn't believe in defunding the police. That they wanted police in their communities and more of a police presence.

I stand with the majority of America. I believe we need police. Since 85% of all Americans believe in having more police, then why are we even talking about defunding police.

You have certain people and organizations that are using it for their own personal agendas. They are adding fuel to the fire for their personal gain. They are also trying to use it to raise racial tensions in America, to help fulfill their own personal agenda. They're advocating this and using the people as their guinea pigs. You're being lied to and used for other people's personal agendas.

As for the rioting on the streets, you may have some gang members that would love nothing more than to have the police removed from their neighborhood. We know what their agenda is, to own and run your neighborhoods. This will not turnout out to be good thing for all the great citizens of this country.

Since the government knows most of the population does not agree with what's happening, why aren't they taking action to stop the rioting. Because they have their own personal agenda, I pointed that out in other chapters, so I won't go over them again.

What it does show, is they don't care about what the majority of America wants. All they care about is their own personal agendas and it proves they don't care about America as a whole. If they did, they would put an end to this nonsense, instead of supporting it.

There's 380 million people in the US. There's a few thousand people that are disrupting our lives and it must come to an end. It's time for the rest of America too voice our opinions and let them know, we don't agree with how they're handling this. They need to stop catering to these small groups and do what's right for the majority.

It's time we let them know, to get these people off our streets. So, the rest of us can live in peace. There's plenty of great people in every neighborhood in America and we all want to live in peace, and go on with our lives, we're tired of the rhetoric.

Oh, if you live somewhere that is not affected by all this chaos, if the police are defunded, it will reach your area. Criminals have no boundaries, eventually they will spread across the country like a plague. The only cure for this disease will be a gun. If we don't put an end to this now, the future of the US will be an all-out war. Anarchy will reign across America.

Lastly, the government has a plan to remove cops from the streets and go to military policing. They will not be doing this to protect you, it will be done to control you. Why do you think they are releasing criminals back onto our streets?

They want total anarchy, so they can step in and take over. They are using everything they can from allowing the riots to continue, releasing criminals, racism, and defunding police to push their agenda.

They're instituting chaos in your neighborhoods, so when they must step in, they will try to look like heroes. Behind the scenes they have a hidden agenda and that's all about controlling America. You're being deceived into falling for it and believing that they have your best interest in mind. It's a huge smoke screen, don't fall for it.

Packing the Supreme Court

One of the best ways for the government to destroy the constitution and control every aspect of your life is to pack the supreme court.

Court packing refers to the process of Congress adding more seats to the Supreme Court to secure a majority.

I won't spend much time on this because the conclusion is simple. When you pack the supreme court, you load it up with one party.

Example is the Democrats want to pack the supreme court in their favor, by adding more seats.

What this accomplishes is a one-sided ruling, making it easier for them to pass any bills that are pushed through.

How does this affect you? If they want to pass laws

to control you or take away your rights, it becomes easy to do. If they want to dismantle or do away with the constitution, they can.

The bottom line is, they can impose any laws onto the people as they see fit. They can change or eliminate the constitution to fit their needs. Having complete control to fulfill their own personal agendas.

The Supreme Court is the last line of defense for protecting the American People. If you allow them to pack it in favor of one side, your life, liberty, and justice are all taken away. It's just that simple.

Downfall of America

As you can see by reading the book, we have a lot of issues in America. Many of these issues will help lead to the downfall of America.

One of the things that will cause a collapse in America is our economy. If we don't learn how to control our spending, we will surely have an economic crisis on our hands. This may seem to be just a monetary issue, but Americans are used to thinking with their pocketbook first.

As I stated in previous chapters, when our taxes are so hi and Americans have less or no money or to spend. This will affect everyone's attitude and will cause angst among many Americans. Not to mention social issues.

The fact is, in the future we face an overpopulation problem in America. As I stated before, overpopulation isn't because you have too many people. It's when you

Americas Future Paying Higher Taxes

don't have enough food to feed them.

When this happens and people don't have enough food to eat, they will go to extreme lengths to feed their family. This includes theft or robbery, and this will surely turn many Americans against each other. If we don't get a handle on how many people are coming into our country, this will happen sooner than later.

The violence in America is growing at a rapid rate. Whether it's racial tensions or protesting in the streets. If these acts continue to go on, there will be fighting amongst everyone at some point. If we don't put an end to it, it will escalate and become a larger problem.

The future of America will look like something from the movie gangs of New York, where everyone has turned against each other and its total chaos. It will reach all communities across America.

America is becoming more and more unrest every day. Tensions are rising across America. The causes of this are uncertainty of what the future holds. Our economy has become more unstable. Racial tensions are rising. More gun violence and unrest in our streets with protests, looting and rioting.

Right now, we have other countries watching what's happening in America and they are just waiting for the opportunity to take over. Whether that's monetarily by buying up our debt or waiting for our country to collapse. So, they can come in and take over our Government.

One of the biggest problems we have in America is, there's certain people and organizations that want our country to collapse. They're doing everything in their power to turn us against each other.

This is not a joking matter; they have the attitude that they want to control the country. They want to control how you live. They want you under their thumb, where they control everything, you do.

There are a couple ways to accomplish this. One way is to run the debt up so high, so when the economy starts to collapse, they can come in and take your paycheck and everything you own and control you financially. Trust me they want it all.

The other way is to turn the people against each other and eventually everything will collapse. When it does, they will come in and take control of every aspect of your life. The words socialism or communism come to mind. They have an agenda, and they will go to great lengths to fulfill it.

Remember, to make this happen easily for them, they need to disarm you. That plan is in place, they are using gun violence and racial tensions as their driving force to fulfill their agenda. The more people they can persuade, the easier it gets for them.

If you thought about these last statements, good for you. Because they are doing it right now. The plan has already been put in place and started.

The only way out of this, is for the American people to come together and let them know that we're not going to tolerate it. That we don't agree with their plan for future America. That we want to decide what the future America looks like.

Americas Future Paying Higher Taxes

If we don't, I picture the future of the United States looking like the movie Mad Max. Where everyone is fighting to survive.

One last thing, we are being fed a pack of lies. We are being fed propaganda, so they can take over and control our lives. They want us under their thumb, so they can control us. To take away our values, freedom, and way of life. We need to stop buying into all the lies they're feeding us and stand up for a great America.

As you can see by reading this book. We have many forces working against us that will not create a good future for America. Our only way out of this is to make changes now. We need to work together to accomplish this, because the future of the United States and life as we know it, are at risk.

The two most important things we need to do is, stop the packing of the courts and we need to protect the constitution. If we don't, they will control every aspect of our lives.

I Wish Everyone the Best of Luck in The Future

Author Information

Thanks for taking time to read my book. If you read any of the books in the America's Future series, there's no sense in reading another. They have a different format, but basically discuss the same topics.

If you have any input or topics, you want me to discuss in my books. You can contact me at.

billygrinslott@gmail.com

Please help by spreading the word about this book. I would be greatly appreciated.

If you could take the time to give me a good review. It would be greatly appreciated.

Thanks.

Billy Grinslott

Copyright © 2021. All rights reserved.

Americas Future Paying Higher Taxes

Americas Future Paying Higher Taxes

www.ingramcontent.com/pod-product-compliance
Lightning Source LLC
Chambersburg PA
CBHW050246220526
45465CB00002B/573